DOVER PUBLICATIONS

Ruthless Rhymes for Heartless Homes
and More Ruthless Rhymes

by

HARRY GRAHAM

DOVER PUBLICATIONS, INC.
Mineola, New York

DOVER THRIFT EDITIONS

GENERAL EDITOR: PAUL NEGRI

12 · 6 · 1

Published in Canada by General Publishing Company, Ltd., 30 Lesmill Road, Don Mills, Toronto, Ontario.

Published in the United Kingdom by Constable and Company, Ltd., 3 The Lanchesters, 162–164 Fulham Palace Road, London W6 9ER.

Bibliographical Note

This Dover edition of *Ruthless Rhymes for Heartless Homes and More Ruthless Rhymes*, first published in 1998, is a slightly altered republication of the works originally published in 1899 and 1930 by Edward Arnold, Ltd.

International Standard Book Number: 0-486-40218-5

Manufactured in the United States of America
Dover Publications, Inc., 31 East 2nd Street, Mineola, N.Y. 11501

CONTENTS

MORE RUTHLESS RHYMES

DEDICATED
TO
MRS W. H. GRENFELL

With the most profound respect,
  I inscribe my dedication,
Realising its effect
  On this volume's circulation;
Since your name can hardly fail
To command a ready sale.

If the sunshine of your smile
  Lights our work, nor wanders off it,
Self and artist in a while
  Hope to share a handsome profit;
But, if you (and Fate) are cross,
Mr. Arnold bears the loss.

Do, I beg you, realise
  Your responsible position,
If this book should ever rise
  To a third or fourth edition;
Understand what you have done
If it fails to weather one!

THE STERN PARENT

Father heard his Children scream,
So he threw them in the stream,
Saying, as he drowned the third,
"Children should be seen, *not* heard!"

1

NURSE'S MISTAKE

Nurse, who peppered baby's face
  (She mistook it for a muffin),
Held her tongue and kept her place,
  "Laying low and sayin' nuffin' ";
Mother, seeing baby blinded,
Said, "Oh, nurse, how absent-minded!"

JIM; OR, THE DEFERRED LUNCHEON PARTY

When the line he tried to cross,
　The express ran into Jim;
Bitterly I mourn his loss —
　I was to have lunched with him.

THE FOND FATHER

Of Baby I was very fond,
  She'd won her father's heart;
So, when she fell into the pond,
  It gave me quite a start.

EQUANIMITY

Aunt Jane observed, the second time
    She tumbled off a bus,
"The step is short from the Sublime
    To the Ridiculous."

TENDER-HEARTEDNESS

Billy, in one of his nice new sashes,
Fell in the fire and was burnt to ashes;
Now, although the room grows chilly,
I haven't the heart to poke poor Billy.

UNSELFISHNESS

All those who see my children say,
  "What sweet, what kind, what charming elves!"
They are so thoughtful, too, for they
  Are *always* thinking of themselves.
It must be ages since I ceased
To wonder which I liked the least.

Such is their generosity,
  That, when the roof began to fall,
They would not share the risk with me,
  But said, "No, father, take it all!"
Yet I should love them more, I know,
If I did not dislike them so.

ECONOMY

My eldest son (his name is Jim)
　　Came up to London and got lost;
I've had to advertise for him —
　　You've no idea how much it cost.

And now, as it does not appear
　　That I shall see my boy again,
I'm sad to think I've wasted near-
　　-Ly £20, and all in vain!

APPRECIATION

Auntie, did you feel no pain
    Falling from that apple tree?
Will you do it, please, again?
    Cos my friend here didn't see.

OBSTRUCTION

You know "Lord's"? Well, once I played there,
    And a ball I hit to leg —
Struck the umpire's head and stayed there,
    As a nest retains an egg.
Hastily the wicket-keeper
    Seized a stump and prized about;

* * *

Had it gone two inches deeper
    He would ne'er have run me out.

* * *

This I minded all the more,
As my stroke was well worth four.

SELF-SACRIFICE

Father, chancing to chastise
  His indignant daughter Sue,
Said, "I hope you realise
  That this hurts me more than you."

Susan straightway ceased to roar;
  "If that's really true," said she,
"I can stand a good deal more;
  Pray go on, and don't mind me."

THE SHARK

Bob was bathing in the Bay,
When a Shark who passed that way
Punctured him in seven places;
— And he made *such* funny faces!

CARELESS JANE

Jane, who shot her Uncle Bill,
 Said his death did not affect her,
But, which makes it sadder still,
 Broke my "hammerless Ejector."

IMPETUOUS SAMUEL

Sam had spirits nought could check,
  And to-day, at breakfast, he
Broke his baby-sister's neck,
  So he shan't have jam for tea!

CALCULATING CLARA

O'er the rugged mountain's brow
    Clara threw the twins she nursed,
And remarked, "I wonder now
    Which will reach the bottom first?"

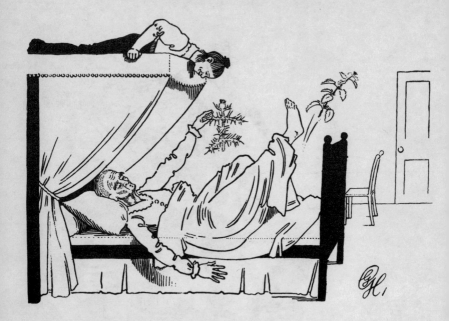

INCONSIDERATE HANNAH

Naughty little Hannah said
   She could make her Grandma whistle,
So, that night, inside her bed
   Placed some nettles and a thistle.

Though dear Grandma quite infirm is,
   Heartless Hannah watched her settle,
With her poor old epidermis
   Resting up against a nettle.

Suddenly she reached the thistle!
My! you should have heard her whistle!

* * *

A successful plan was Hannah's,
But I cannot praise her manners.

16

MR. JONES

"There's been an accident!" they said,
"Your servant's cut in half; he's dead!"
"Indeed!" said Mr. Jones, "and please
Send me the half that's got my keys."
G. W.

SCORCHING JOHN

John, who rode his Dunlop tyre
O'er the head of sweet Maria,

When she writhed in frightful pain,
Had to blow it out again.

PHILIP

Philip, foozling with his cleek,
Drove his ball through Helen's cheek;

Sad they bore her corpse away,
Seven up and six to play.

H. J. L. G.

MISFORTUNES NEVER COME SINGLY

Making toast at fireside,
Nurse fell in the grate and died;

And, what makes it ten times worse,
All the toast was burned *with* nurse.

THE PERILS OF OBESITY

Yesterday my gun exploded
When I thought it wasn't loaded;
Near my wife I pressed the trigger,
Chipped a fragment off her figure,

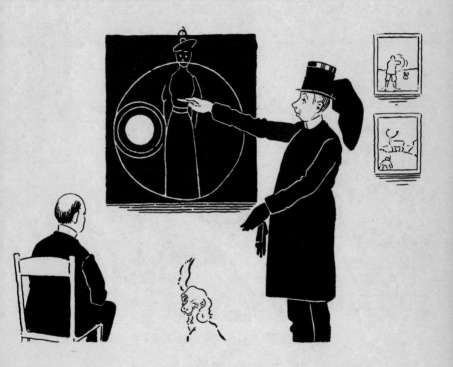

'Course I'm sorry, and all that,
But she shouldn't be so fat.

AUNT ELIZA

In the drinking-well
   Which the plumber built her,
Aunt Eliza fell . . . .

. . . . We must buy a filter.

THE CHILDREN'S "DON'T"

I.

Don't tell Papa his nose is red
    As any rosebud or geranium,
Forbear to eye his hairless head
    Or criticise his cootlike cranium;
'Tis years of sorrow and of care
Have made his head come through his hair.

THE CHILDREN'S "DON'T"

II.

Don't give your endless guinea-pig
  (Wherein that animal may build a
Sufficient nest) the Sunday wig
  Of poor, dear, dull, deaf Aunt Matilda.
Oh, *don't* tie strings across her path,
Or empty beetles in her bath!

THE CHILDREN'S "DON'T"

III.

Don't ask your uncle why he's fat;
　Avoid upon his toe-joints treading;
Don't hide a hedgehog in his hat,
　Or bury brushes in his bedding.
He will not see the slightest sport
In pepper put into his port!

THE CHILDREN'S "DON'T"

IV.

Don't pull away the cherished chair
　On which Mamma intended sitting,
Nor yet prepare her session there
　By setting on the seat her knitting;
Pause ere you hurt her spine, I pray —
That is a game that *two* can play.

More Ruthless Rhymes

for Heartless Homes

By

Harry Graham

Illustrated by

Ridgewell

LONDON: EDWARD ARNOLD & CO.

INDIFFERENCE

When Grandmamma fell off the boat,
And couldn't swim (and wouldn't float),
Matilda just stood by and smiled.
I almost could have slapped the child.

PROVIDENCE

Fate moves in a mysterious way,
   As shown by Uncle Titus,
Who unexpectedly, one day,
   Was stricken with St. Vitus.
It proved a blessing in disguise,
   For, thanks to his condition,
He won the Non-Stop Dancing Prize
   At Wembley Exhibition.

CONSOLATION

I sliced a brassey-shot at Rye,
And killed a luckless passer-by.
The ball rebounded off his head
And, landing on the green, lay dead.
His widow it must much console
To know 'twas thus I won the hole.

TRAGEDY

That morning, when my wife eloped
With James, our chauffeur, how I moped!
What tragedies in life there are!
I'm dashed if I can start the car!

PRESENCE OF MIND

When, with my little daughter Blanche,
  I climbed the Alps, last summer,
I saw a dreadful avalanche
  About to overcome her;
And, as it swept her down the slope,
  I vaguely wondered whether
I should be wise to cut the rope
  That held us twain together.

* * *

I must confess I'm glad I did,
But still I miss the child — poor kid!

COMPENSATION

Weep not for little Léonie,
Abducted by a French *Marquis!*
Though loss of honour was a wrench,
Just think how it's improved her French!

DISCIPLINE

To Percival, my youngest son,
Who cut his sister's throat, for fun,
I said: "Now, Percy! Manners, please!
You really mustn't be a tease!
I shall refuse, another time,
To take you to the Pantomime!"

OBSTINACY

I warned poor Mary of her fate,
But she *would* wed a plumber's mate!
For hours the choir was forced to sing
While he went back to fetch the ring.

UPLIFT

It seems that with Eternal Youth
   Great-Grandmamma is gifted,
For though (to tell the honest truth)
   Her face has twice been "lifted,"
To-day she doesn't look to me
A minute more than ninety-three.

CARELESSNESS

A window-cleaner in our street
Who fell (five storeys) at my feet
Impaled himself on my umbrella.
I said: "Come, come, you careless fella!
If my umbrella had been shut
You might have landed on my nut!"

L'ENFANT GLACÉ

When Baby's cries grew hard to bear
I popped him in the Frigidaire.
I never would have done so if
I'd known that he'd be frozen stiff.
My wife said: "George, I'm so unhappé!
Our darling's now completely *frappé!*"

WINTER SPORTS

The ice upon our pond's so thin
That poor Mamma has fallen in!
We cannot reach her from the shore
Until the surface freezes more.
Ah me, my heart grows weary waiting —
Besides, I want to have some skating.

THOUGHTLESSNESS

I never shall forget my shame
To find my son had forged my name.
If he'd had any thought for others
He might at least have forged his mother's.

OPPORTUNITY

When Mrs. Gorm (Aunt Eloïse)
Was stung to death by savage bees,
Her husband (Prebendary Gorm)
Put on his veil, and took the swarm.
He's publishing a book, next May,
On "How to Make Bee-keeping Pay."

LORD GORBALS

Once, as old Lord Gorbals motored
  Round his moors near John o' Groats,
He collided with a goatherd
  And a herd of forty goats.
By the time his car got through
They were all defunct but two.

Roughly he addressed the goatherd:
  "Dash my whiskers and my corns!
Can't you teach your goats, you dotard,
  That they ought to sound their horns?
Look, my A.A. badge is bent!
I've a mind to raise your rent!"

LONDON CALLING

When rabies attacked my Uncle Daniel,
And he had fits of barking like a spaniel,
The B.B.C. relayed him (from all stations)
At *Children's Hour* in "farmyard imitations."

QUIET FUN

My son Augustus, in the street, one day,
  Was feeling quite exceptionally merry.
A stranger asked him: "Can you show me, pray,
  The quickest way to Brompton Cemetery?"
"The quickest way? You bet I can!" said Gus,
  And pushed the fellow underneath a bus.

* * *

Whatever people say about my son,
He does enjoy his little bit of fun.

THRIFT

Last week our Parlourmaid withdrew
   Her savings from the Bank,
And sailed away to far Peru.
   Next day, her vessel sank!
She perished in an upper bunk,
And thus her sinking-fund was sunk.

THE LAST STRAW

Oh, gloomy, gloomy was the day
When poor Aunt Bertha ran away!
But Uncle finds to-day more black:
Aunt Bertha's threatening to run back!

BULL'S-EYE

At rifle-practice on the sands at Deal,
I fired at what I took to be a seal.
When later on I learnt 'twas sister Florrie
And that I'd shot her, I was very sorry.
But still it gratified me just a trifle
To find myself so expert with a rifle,
For, with so large a target as my sister,
I should have been a duffer if I'd missed her.

GRANDPAPA

Grandpapa fell down a drain;
Couldn't scramble out again.
Now he's floating down the sewer
There's one grandpapa the fewer.

WASTE

Our governess—would you believe
It?—drowned herself on Christmas Eve!
This was a waste, as, any way,
It would have been a holiday.

BISHOP PROUT

In Burma, once, while Bishop Prout
  Was preaching on Predestination,
There came a sudden waterspout
  And drowned the congregation.
"O Heav'n!" he cried, "why can't you wait
Until they've handed round the plate?"

CANON GLOY

One morning, just as Canon Gloy
　　Was starting gaily for the station,
The Doctor said: "Your eldest boy
　　Must have another operation!"
"What!" cried the Canon. "Not again?
That's *twice* he's made me miss my train!"

PATIENCE

When ski-ing in the Engadine
My hat blew off down a ravine.
My son, who went to fetch it back,
Slipped through an icy glacier's crack
And then got permanently stuck.
It really was infernal luck:
My hat was practically new—
I loved my little Henry too—
And I may have to wait for years
Till either of them reappears.